Photo: Aparna Nori

DEEPIKA ARWIND

Deepika Arwind is an international playwright and theatre-maker originally from Bangalore whose work has been presented across India, the USA and Europe. She has won or been nominated for several awards, including the Toto Award, the Rolex Mentor and Protégé Arts Initiative, and The Hindu Playwright Award.

She was recently a playwright-in-residence at Jagriti, part of The International Conference of Insecurity – a collective of performers from eight countries based in Zurich (2022), and playwright-in-residence for the Welt/Buehne season at the Residenztheater in Munich.

She will be a fellow at the Akademie Schloss Solitude in Stuttgart for most of 2023.

First published in the UK in 2023 by Aurora Metro Publications Ltd.

80 Hill Rise, Richmond, TW10 6UB

www.aurorametro.com   info@aurorametro.com

X:@aurorametro FB: /AuroraMetroBooks

Phantasmagoria © Deepika Arwind, 2023

Cover design copyright Aurora Metro Books © 2023

Editing & Production: Cheryl Robson

Printed in the UK by 4edge Ltd, Essex on sustainably resourced paper.

ISBNs:

978-1-911501-18-3 (print)

978-1-911501-19-0 (ebook)

PHANTASMAGORIA

BY

DEEPIKA ARWIND

AURORA METRO BOOKS

CONTENTS

Kali Theatre develops and presents thought provoking, contemporary new plays by South Asian women which reflect and comment on our lives today. Kali's award-winning productions have won rave reviews, sell out performances and inspired audiences throughout the UK and beyond.

Find out more and join their mailing list at

www.kalitheatre.co.uk

To mark their 30th birthday, Methuen published THIRTY, a book of extracts from many of the ground-breaking plays they have presented over the past 30 years. You can find the book and many of the scripts for sale at the online Kali Script Shop on their website.

Cast in order of appearance

Scherezade – Ulrika Krishnamurti
Mehrosh – Hussina Raja
Jai – Antony Bunsee
Bina – Tania Rodrigues

Writer – Deepika Arwind
Director – Jo Tyabji
Artistic Producer – Helena Bell
Consultant Designer – Miriam Nabarro
Designer – Roisin Martindale
Lighting Designer – Neill Brinkworth
Sound Designer – Dinah Mullen
Video Designer – Gillian Tan
Assistant Director – Skye Hallam
Dramaturg – Nic Wass
Production Manager – Crin Claxton
Costume Supervisor – Eve Oakley
Company Stage Manager – Joe Colgan
ASM – Rhea Cosford

Fight Consultant – RC-Annie
Set built by Set Blue Scenery
Video trailer by Tom Paul Martin
Captioning service at selected performances by Stagetext

A reading of an earlier version of *Phantasmagoria* was presented as part of Kali's *International Plays* week in March 2023

Thanks to all the actors who have taken part in the development workshops for *Phantasmagoria*.

The development of *Phantasmagoria* was supported by the National Theatre Studio Generate Programme.

Supported using public funding by
**ARTS COUNCIL
ENGLAND**

The Generate Programme

**National
Theatre**

Jo Tyabji – *Director*

Jo Tyabji is a writer and director of theatre and performance. Recent work includes Inua Ellam's *Antigone* at Regents Park Open Air Theatre, co-directed with Max Webster, *Marty and The Party* by Luke Skilbeck at the Queen Elizabeth Hall and national tour, *Rise* by Zia Ahmed for Kiln Theatre, and immersive audio adventure *One Christmas Wish,* adapted by Anna Wheatley from the book by Katherine Rundell, which toured in Graphite & Diamond's mobile venue The Palace. Buzzcut, Milk Presents, and Now Press Play have produced her writing for audio. Jo is Creative Director of Graphite & Diamond and Associate Director at Milk Presents.

Hussina Raja – *Mehrosh*

Plays new regular role 'Nida' in the latest series of *Man Like Mobeen* for Tiger Aspect/BBC and can soon be seen in BBC Films independent feature *In Camera* directed by Naqqash Khalid, alongside Nabhaan Rizwan. Previously Hussina played 'Aminah' opposite Riz Ahmed in *The Long Goodbye*, an Oscar, Cannes and BIFA award-winning short, directed by Aneil Karia. Feature work includes independent films *A Moving Image*, directed by Shola Amoo and BAFTA-nominated *The Survivalist* with Mia Goth. Television includes: Disney+ comedy *Back To Life*, Bad Wolf's *A Discovery Of Witches* and *Informer* for Amazon Prime, and *Hansa* in ITV's *The Level.*

Antony Bunsee – *Jai*

Graduated from Bristol Old Vic. Recent theatre includes *The Comedy of Errors* (Royal Shakespeare Company), *Lidless* (Trafalgar Studios), Kite Runner (Wyndhams and on tour), *The Histories* and *Midnight's Children* (RSC) and as The Count in *Dracula* (Derby Playhouse). Recent screenwork includes *Foundation* (Apple TV), *Doctor Strange 2, Catherine Called Birdy, Sex and the City 2, Hollyoaks* and *Eastenders*. A regular on BBC World Services' Westway, Antony has also voiced The Hafiz in *Tumanbey* (Radio 4).

Ulrika Krishnamurti – *Scherezade*

Ulrika trained at Guildford School of Acting. Theatre includes: *Lotus Beauty* (Hampstead Theatre); *Satyagraha* (Improbable/English National Opera); *Around the World in 80 Days* (York Theatre Royal); *Checkpoint Chana* (Finborough Theatre); *Pink Sari Revolution* (Belgrade/ Curve/ WYP/ Northern Stage); *Made in India* (Soho Theatre/ UK National Tour); *Echoes Within Walls* (Solo Festival); *Commencing* (Tristan Bates Theatre); *Twelve* (Kali Theatre); *Mahabharata* (Sutradhar). Film includes: *The Anushree Experiments*; *London Paris New York*; *Rockford*. TV includes: *Casualty, Holby City* and *That's English*.

Tania Rodrigues – *Bina*

Since graduating from Drama Studio London Tania Rodrigues has worked extensively in theatre, screen and audio. Her theatre appearances include *Midnight's Children* (Royal Shakespeare Company), *Croydon Avengers* (Ovalhouse), *Heer Ranjha* (Tramway), *Romeo & Juliet* (Orange Tree), *Robin Hood* (Stratford East). Her onscreen appearances include *Rev, Liar, Cuckoo, Eastenders, Doctors, Holby City, Silent Witness, Casualty, A Nice Arrangement, Lovejoy, Inspector Morse, Coronation Street*, and *Oranges Are Not The Only Fruit*. As a voice artist, she has narrated over a hundred audiobooks by many award-winning authors and has recently voiced the new animated *In The Night Garden* series.

Roisin Martindale – *Designer*

Roisin works as a Set and Costume Designer based in South London and graduated with an MA in Performance Design from Bristol Old Vic Theatre School in 2019. Past Design Work includes: *Bitter Lemons* (Pleasance Beneath, Edinburgh Fringe/Bristol Old Vic - Weston Studio); *I am England* and *Blood Wedding* (The Egg Theatre, Bath, 2023); *Never Not Once* (Park Theatre 90, 2022). Assistant/ Associate Work includes: *Disruption* (Park Theatre 200, London); *Sweeney Todd* (The Egg Theatre, Bath); Design Associate on *Big Big Sky* (Hampstead Theatre). Exhibition work includes: *Hallyu! The Korean Wave* (V&A, London).

Neill Brinkworth – *Lighting Designer*

Lighting Designer for a wide range of plays, musicals, opera & dance. Previously for Kali: *Noor;* Recent credits include: *The Flying Dutchman* (Opera Up Close); *Don Giovanni* (Greek National Opera); *Cinema Inferno* (Imitating the Dog); *Afterite* revival (Wayne McGregor, La Scala, Milan); *Ghostbusters* (Secret Cinema); *Katya Kabanova* revival (Teatro dell'opera, Rome); *Merrily We Roll Along, Spring Awakening* (Leeds Conservatoire); *The Girl on the Train* (English Theatre Frankfurt); *Alice's Adventures Underground* (Irish National Opera);*The Dark* (Fuel Theatre); *Jekyll & Hyde* (Chester Storyhouse); *Hansel & Gretel* revival (San Francisco Opera); *In the Night Garden Live* (Minor Entertainment); *Blank* (NT Connections, Dorfmann Theatre); *The Firm* (Hampstead Theatre); *Dessa Rose* (Trafalgar Studios).

Gillian Tan – *Video Designer*

Theatre: *A Playlist for the Revolution* (Bush Theatre), *South Pacific* (Chichester & Tour); *Mind Mangler* (Mischief); *Stars* (ICA & Tour); *The Body Remembers* (Fuel), *Black Love* (Paines Plough & Belgrade Theatre); *Really Big & Really Loud* (Paines Plough/Belgrade Theatre); *Cinderella* (Polka), *Alyssa, Memoirs of A Queen* (Vaudeville Theatre); *Aisha and Abhaya* (Royal Ballet/ Rambert); *Majestique* (Skråen); *The Song Project – Is In Our Blood* (Royal Court); *4.48 Psychosis* (Lyric Hammersmith/Royal Opera); *La Soirée* (Aldwych/ Southbank/Skråen); *Coraline* (Barbican/Royal Opera); *Tamburlaine* (Arcola); *Invisible Treasure* (Ovalhouse); *Who Do We Think We Are* (Southwark Playhouse); *Crocodiles* (Royal Exchange, Manchester). Film credits: *Deep England, Held Momentarily* (RAM)

Dinah Mullen – *Sound Designer*

Dinah is a performance sound artist and designer for live and digital performance; specialising in dance, interactive storytelling and devising. Recent Theatre credits include *Squirrel* (The Unicorn, dir. Tim Bell), *Attempts on Her Life* (Tobacco Factory, dir. Kalungi Ssebandeke), *Icarus* (Tobacco Factory, dir. Nancy Medina), *Owl at Home* (Welsh Tour, dir. Lee Lyford). Recent Other: *Forge* (Performance Installation @ Transform Festival, Barbican Pit), *Unit 15 for MAYK* (Horizon Showcase, Edinburgh, Dir. Rachel Mars/Wendy Hubbard), *With Fire and Rage* (Interactive Audio Walk for Eurofestival Liverpool, Dir. Zoe Lafferty), *Ministry of Time Travel* (Smart phone based adventure for The National Archives, Coney).

Miriam Nabarro – *Consultant designer*

Miriam Nabarro is a UK based scenographer and artist. Current projects include *At the Forest's Edge* (RSC), *The Wild Hunt of King Stakh* (Belarus Free Theatre/Barbican) and *High Times, Dirty Monsters* (20 Stories High/Graeae). She has designed over 40 productions including *Stars* by M. Adebayo (Tamasha/ ICA), award-winning *The Great Game, Afghanistan* (Tricycle + US), *Dr Korczacs Example* (Royal Exchange), *Palace of the End* (Royal Exchange, Traverse). Miriam is the Creative Associate for 20 Stories High and a regular artist with Clean Break. She is artist-in-residence at SOAS, her visual work is held in many collections (inter)nationally.

www.miriamnabarro.co.uk

ABOUT THE PLAY
By Deepika Arwind

I started writing *Phantasmagoria* with the intention that begins most of my work – a conversation with the questions we're confronted with while living in a very precarious world. I felt like no matter where I was, the ability to simply talk about difficult things was dramatically decreasing. We were either screaming or shutting each other down. We were certainly unable to listen. So I began writing a play that investigated this phenomenon and it revealed to me what was underneath: a deep grief and a deep, deep fear.

How do we talk and debate and argue with each other across the manufactured sharp edges we're made to believe we occupy? While we're fractured on every level of public and private life, living inside a climate emergency and through ongoing wars, could being in a theatre be a safer space to look this fear, this grief, in the eyes? To think of what makes us afraid and why? How does fear lodge itself in our bodies and what can it make us do?

What does a stage on which we're really confronted with ourselves look like?

Phantasmagoria is an invitation to 'see' despite the overwhelming folds of darkness we're currently inhabiting. I hope *Phantasmagoria* makes us think about the person we most disagree with – and perhaps even measure the distance between us. I hope we think about what it might mean to walk it.

Why are some people more human than others and what does power have to do with this accordance of humanity? What is the legacy of power we're at peace with to inherit?

I hope it makes us consider the natural world, and our relationship to everything 'outside' of ourselves. I hope it makes us *feel* our complicity and activism, our nonchalance and our opinions, our courage and our simultaneous cowardice.

I'll be honest: I'm not terribly hopeful about the world right now. I'm aware that's a rather dismal opinion for anyone – especially an artist – to express. I know the work is to *find* the hope, to excavate it from places it doesn't live in.

But with this play I've been interested in first contouring the dismay I feel. And in some way to reason with it. With this map laid out naked in front of me – of us – we can start to think of what the path out of the darkness looks like.

PHANTASMAGORIA

Deepika Arwind

First performed by Kali Theatre at Belgrade Theatre, Coventry on October 5th, 2023. Directed by Jo Tyabji.

The characters in this play are fictional. Any resemblance to anyone living or dead is purely coincidental.

Characters:

SCHEREZADE – A young woman, aged 25. She is the Personal Assistant to the Deputy Leader of a fictional ruling party. She has a particular way of speaking that is written into the script. She wears gloves.

MEHROSH – A young woman, aged around 28. Her body is athletic, her manner composed, her speech carefully weighed. She is the president of a fictional student union of a fictional university.

BINA – A woman; 45-50 years. Very well-dressed, well-put together, distinct. The Deputy Leader of a fictional ruling political party.

JAI – A journalist; 45-50 years. A senior TV journalist who used to be with a major fictional news channel. Now independent.

Acts and Scenes

There is a deliberate choice to have the play unfold in a contained space without the division of scenes and acts.

This is a decision related to form that one hopes will be clear as the play unfolds.

Setting:

The play is set in an imaginary country slightly in the future. Interior is a kind of green room, ostensibly, in a summer house in the capital, although we only ever see the room. The room is mostly tasteful but not too put together, as it hasn't been used in a long time. The room overlooks a forest, referred to as the sprawling green, which can be seen through a large glass window. One can determine the time of the day through this outside view.

There are other elements in the room such as:

- a pillar in the centre of the room

- two chairs

- a dressing table with mirrors

- a bathroom door

- and a sofa / couch.

- a fridge and a kettle station

These can be suitably designed for the text.

Perhaps a painting and cloth lamp are part of the design too.

The shadow play with lights is quite important, and uses the idea of shadows employed in horror theatre.

Time:

Early evening to night. In the impending hours before a live debate MEHROSH, a fictional student activist and BINA, the spokesperson from a fictional ruling party, meet in a summer house outside the city for the first time. Pitched as adversaries – political and ideological – and brought together by a common journalist friend, they sit in a liminal space, an ante-room of sorts – waiting. Eerie happenings – creatures and shadows in the dark, haunt this time, a 'theatre of horror' begins to play out inside the dressing room.

Notes:

'/' denotes where speech or action has been interrupted by someone else

'-' means a break in speech

SCHEREZADE walks through the door, with earphones and looking at a video on her phone. She nearly walks into the pillar. Doesn't pause her video. Surveys the room briefly. Looks outside for a moment and sits on the floor leaning on the pillar, still watching the video. Nods off to sleep.

A few moments later MEHROSH enters. SCHEREZADE is not in her view. MEHROSH removes the layers of her clothing one by one. It's a slow and deliberate process. She folds each item of clothing carefully. Underneath she is in a vest and tights. She is clearly athletic.

She looks across to the large glass window overlooking the sprawling green, still unaware of SCHEREZADE's presence. Stares out for a while as she massages her legs a bit. She begins to stretch - folding forward, downward dog.

After a few moments, MEHROSH is on her hands in a handstand and she tries to walk in the handstand. She is unable to do so, but she comes back to standing with complete grace. She goes into child's pose, breathing loudly.

SCHEREZADE wakes up to realise MEHROSH is in the room. She watches her intently. MEHROSH gets out of child's pose. Goes back into a handstand. Manages to take two steps on her hands. These are neat and precise movements.

MEHROSH gets back down and sees SCHEREZADE peering out from behind the pillar. They look at each other for a few moments, quite blankly. Two creatures blinking. MEHROSH puts on another layer to cover her arms.

MEHROSH   Sorry, I didn't see you.

SCHEREZADE   Me too. I was sleeping. Sorry. (*Pause*) I got up too early, that's why.

MEHROSH (*pointing to the sofa*) You can use this if you want.

SCHEREZADE   Thanks, but I don't like sleeping on sofa.

MEHROSH   All right.

SCHEREZADE You can continue your - exercise ma'am, no problem. (*Pause*) I'm waiting for my boss. (*Pause*) Bina ma'am is my boss. She must be stuck in the traffic outside the city.

MEHROSH   Oh, I see. So you are her –

SCHEREZADE   PA. Personal Assistant.

MEHROSH   –

SCHEREZADE   My official designation is PA, but we can call it Personal Association. I am her right-hand, basically. Also friend. Not BFF but very close.

Pause.

MEHROSH   Do you know what time she will be here?

SCHEREZADE   I can check it out, ma'am. I have to call her, anyway. Actually, no, if she is stuck in traffic she will be meditating and if I disturb that... Sorry, I won't call her.

MEHROSH continues stretching.

MEHROSH   Doesn't sound like an almost-BFF situation to me.

SCHEREZADE   Bina ma'am is just *too* particular about everything. You know, her routine and her best practices. Mmm... I think so I will message her two-hand-joined emojis saying come fast, ma'am, the debate can't start without you. *(Pause)* How you came, ma'am? I mean to here, not into this world.

MEHROSH smiles.

MEHROSH   Jai sir sent me a car. I didn't expect it to be this far out of the city.

SCHEREZADE   Yes, I haven't been here before even though it is Bina ma'am's property. So good of her to let Jai sir use it for this event, no?

Pause. MEHROSH tries not to look surprised.

SCHEREZADE   They haven't done much events in this place. Or maybe ever.

MEHROSH   I can see why.

SCHEREZADE   Ma'am said it used to be nice when it was just their summer house.

MEHROSH goes into child's pose, aware that SCHEREZADE is watching her. As MEHROSH stretches in child's pose, the door opens briefly. JAI's voice is heard.

JAI   Sorry. I think Mehrosh is doing her prayers. Let's give her a few minutes to finish. By the way, the light is magnificent in this room.

MEHROSH and SCHEREZADE smile at each other.

MEHROSH My prayers... Okay, last ditch attempt.

MEHROSH tries to get into a handstand. Once she is stable on her hands she tries walking. SCHEREZADE records this on her phone casually. MEHROSH in one swift swoop comes down and sits right in front of SCHEREZADE who is taken aback.

MEHROSH   Hey! I saw that!

SCHEREZADE   What...? I...

MEHROSH   Delete it, please. Immediately.

SCHEREZADE   Ma'am, really!

MEHROSH   Please *delete* it. Sorry, I don't even know your name.

SCHEREZADE   Scherezade.

Pause

MEHROSH   Scherezade, please delete it *now*. This isn't a joke.

MEHROSH stares at SCHEREZADE's phone as SCHEREZADE hesitantly deletes the video on her phone.

SCHEREZADE   I wasn't going to do anything with it, ma'am, I just thought it was so cool how you can walk on your/

MEHROSH   You still cannot! How is it okay? Stay, stay behind the pillar please.

SCHEREZADE retreats behind the pillar. MEHROSH puts on each of her layers slowly.

SCHEREZADE   It wasn't in a bad way.

MEHROSH *(sharply)* I don't see what's good about it.

SCHEREZADE   I have to call Bina ma'am.

SCHEREZADE goes into the bathroom and shuts the door with emphasis. MEHROSH walks to the large window to look at the sprawling green. The light changes mildly, and she hears the cry of what sounds like a large cat, which startles her. She continues looking outside to spot the animal. MEHROSH is frozen. After a few moments, Jai enters.

JAI   Hello, my dear Mehrosh. And how are we doing today?

He leans to her for a hug. MEHROSH hugs him, though distractedly, still staying with the sound of the cat.

MEHROSH   I am okay... very tired... Actually, it's been a long week.

JAI   Of course, burning the midnight oil while trying to change the world in the day. Tall order, but we must do what we must do, right?

Pause

MEHROSH   Haven't you given up expecting answers to rhetorical questions?

JAI   We never give up my dear. Hence this debate.

MEHROSH *(sighs)* This debate...

JAI   Exactly, M. But I want more enthusiasm, fervour... the quintessential fire only you can light a space up with/

MEHROSH Jai sir, I can't take you seriously when you go into motivational speaker mode.

JAI   This is your moment to show what you're made of. Public life demands that David stand with conviction in front of Goliath. I know the prospect is intimidating but you must say what you think.

MEHROSH I'm not intimidated, sir. I *am* wondering.. just not sure if this is the right platform.

JAI   You'd rather be on TV? Come on, Mehrosh, if you're looking at a future in politics/

MEHROSH That's *your* vision for me, Jai sir/

JAI   Okay, policy, law, civil administration ... I don't know!

MEHROSH Exactly, you don't. Why didn't you mention this place is such a distance from the city?

JAI   What summer house is *in* the city? *(Referring to her eyes)* We might have to get you a little make-up, M.

MEHROSH Only if you'll get some too, J.

JAI   Atta Girl! Okay, listen, Bina will be here any second. You'll be okay, yes? She doesn't bite, I promise.

MEHROSH But I might. Listen, her PA just *recorded* me. Can you believe it? *(Laughs.)*

JAI   What? *(Pause)* Wait, what? / I can get that fixed.

MEHROSH I took care of it, obviously.

JAI Good God, that's absurd!

MEHROSH It's outrageous, don't you think? These people –

JAI I find her a bit – a bit – is she here?

MEHROSH points to the bathroom.

JAI Bina seems to think she is a dutiful soldier to her, but frankly I don't understand... I forget her name.

MEHROSH Scherezade.

JAI Right – that's an unusual name/

SCHEREZADE comes out of the bathroom.

SCHEREZADE Hello, Mr. Jai. We met at the dinner.

JAI Yes, I remember. We were just talking about you...

SCHEREZADE Yes, I heard my name, so I came –

JAI We were talking about a private matter/

SCHEREZADE I will go back.

SCHEREZADE goes back inside and closes the door.

JAI She's a trip!

They move to the far end of the room.

JAI Okay, now seriously, M. You're good for this evening, yeah?

MEHROSH I don't know if I can be more prepared honestly. I know everything about her now – her favourite colour, her favourite food, favourite holiday destination.

JAI   Then you know what a terrific deflector Bina is...

MEHROSH Especially in her own home I'm sure she's very, very comfortable. Another little thing you forgot to mention?

JAI   Ah yes, but it's hardly important/

MEHROSH How is that *not* important?

JAI   Look, it's a place that's not on many people's radar. My dream for the debate to be live, in an equal, democratic space, not a TV studio/

MEHROSH It's already unequal. I'm on her turf/

JAI   Are you going to be on the backfoot because of a *venue*, Mehrosh /

MEHROSH A venue which happens to be surrounded by a very thick, very dense forest.

JAI   Fine, let's go somewhere else then.

MEHROSH I am saying we share the kind of relation-ship – *I think* – where you could've mentioned who this place belongs to.

JAI   Okay, I'm sorry, I guess? I had a lot of things on my mind, and we've got you here now, so can we please –

MEHROSH I saw her on TV last night coolly replying to a very angry journalist – your friend, I think – who was calling every single person on the panel unpatriotic.

JAI   Don't lump me with that kind of journalist, please.

MEHROSH You're all part of the circus.

JAI Yes, but some of us have made better choices now. To do things well. We're going to upload this after the event, and give people a template of how good debate is done. *(Pause)* When people hear what an articulate, eloquent, young activist you are, you'll see it's worth it.

MEHROSH I'm an ordinary student. The rest are your labels and not my responsibility.

JAI You're not ordinary. I see how many people now think of themselves as *citizens* because of you. I mean one million young people came out of their homes across the country/

MEHROSH I'm doing what many young people have done in the past. And there is nothing wrong with ordinariness, may I remind you, Jai sir.

JAI I've told you M, call me Jai, for god's sake.

MEHROSH It's just that the words student and activist have become pejoratives these days, Jai.

JAI Exactly, change the narrative, yeah? *(Pause)* Bina is a formidable opponent. But she is balanced when it comes to debate – we did it often in college and even now, sometimes at the Cricket Club we banter and she never fails to stimulate me. Look, do this. Do this well. You'll see she has something to offer.

Pause

MEHROSH I wonder if people get tired of posturing as they grow older.

JAI Are you calling me old?

MEHROSH I'm thinking aloud and you're taking it personally.

They smile. Bina enters. For a moment, the three of them stand looking at each other.

SCHEREZADE comes out.

SCHEREZADE   Yes, Mimi. We already discussed two looks for ma'am's photo shoot. One is very clean, very pastel for a rural visit, and other maybe more luxurious, for an evening time event such as cocktails. Actually, high tea. Please revert back to me with options. *(Hangs up)* Hello ma'am. I was in the bathroom for privacy reasons, but I got a feeling you had entered this room.

Pause

BINA   Who is taking what, personally?

MEHROSH We're just joking.

(BINA's phone rings. She cuts the call. Hands the phone to Scherezade.)

BINA   The minister. He can wait. *(extending hand to Mehrosh)* Bina, nice to meet you.

JAI   You haven't met?

MEHROSH We haven't met in person.

BINA   Except as boxes on TV...

SCHEREZADE Last on 24th of last month, ma'm. 9 pm primetime news on *News Today*.

JAI   Ah of course, my former show.

BINA   When you said we have lost our moral compass?

MEHROSH That was me, yes.

Pause.

BINA   No harm, no foul. I appreciate strong opinions... when they're backed by facts.

MEHROSH I have several of those for you, tonight.

BINA   Good, I look forward to sparring with you in an educated way.

MEHROSH The pleasure is mine, ma'am.

BINA   Call me Bina. I've always told Jai how bright I think you are.

JAI   She was full of praises for you while you were doing your prayers.

MEHROSH That's nice to hear, ma'am, from a senior politician such as you. I'm only just finding out you both go back a long way.

BINA   Well, how do you think he got me to do this?

MEHROSH Good to know where we all stand.

BINA   I stand on the ground, my dear. Where the people live. Hopefully so do you.

JAI   Well, here we are ladies. Friends, about to go into a friendly debate, with structure and decency. I told Mehrosh we'd have such interesting debates in university/

SCHEREZADE   Will there be a prize at the end?

BINA   Don't be ridiculous, Sherezade.

SCHEREZADE   Sorry ma'am, I just thought/

BINA   I've told you not to think too much. Could you please tell the team what they should be doing?

SCHEREZADE starts texting the team.

JAI   Now, can we take a moment to discuss how this will play out? *(Pause)* Yes?

BINA   When you don't hear an answer, Jai, it's your cue to continue. *(to MEHROSH)* Men, I tell you.

Bina and MEHROSH share a smile.

JAI   Okay, we're smiling, even if it is at my expense/

BINA   Even top level meetings are like this. Go on Jai.

JAI   Okay, first, I want to thank you both for doing this. I know it's no easy thing for busy women like you to be here spending your evening doing a private event like this. I really, really appreciate it and you.

BINA   Tell us something we don't know.

JAI   Join me in a moment of sentimentality, will you, Bina? *(Pause)* I want to remind you both, and you Scherezade, that we are keeping this quiet for the moment. So no socials until we're uploaded, okay? *(Keeps looking at Scherezade until she nods.)* All right. How we'll begin: I will introduce my new online channel, the idea of good, clean, live debate and how this is the first in a long series. Introduce you both, wait for the cheering that will follow/

BINA   Don't forget to thank your sponsors.

MEHROSH Your sponsors?

JAI   Ah yes, of course. It's on my notes. Then, opening statements. First Bina, then Mehrosh – I used alphabetical order to keep it fair – Okay? Okay! Five minutes each. And when I mean five, I mean five, yeah? You'll hear a bell at four minutes and then a longer bell at five. You go back to your seats when you hear it. Okay? Okay? *(They nod.)* Next, I will ask you guys questions on four topics broadly – the ones I sent you.

SCHEREZADE   Yes, ma'am wants two of them to be replaced. I think that Environment Protection thing, and the other one *(checks her phone)* that secretarianism/

BINA   Sectarianism/

MEHROSH   What? Why?

BINA   Why flare fires where there are none? Besides, we don't start a new series on Jai's new channel by creating unnecessary controversies. We want to support him, yes?

JAI   I – I – Look I think –

BINA   Jai, please. Tell us how the rest will go.

MEHROSH   How is this a fair debate if one of the speakers will decide what topics are up for discussion?

JAI   Mehrosh, can we park that for now, and can I just/

MEHROSH   Fine, go ahead.

JAI   So my questions and your responses will last about forty minutes. You can then ask each other follow-up questions. You will have notepads and pens on your podiums if you need them. Good?

Silence.

JAI   I'll take that as a yes. And then closing statements – if we have time we'll do one question for each of you from the audience. And don't worry, very friendly, highly curated audience so there won't be dumb questions. If not, we say our thank yous, one more round to the sponsors – please appreciate my due diligence Bina – and then we have drinks and dinner.

MEHROSH I need to leave right after the debate. I have an exam to study for.

JAI   Sure, okay, I'll make sure my car is waiting for you/

BINA   That's a pity, Mehrosh. There were some people I wanted to introduce you to. Please stay, let's break bread together. *(Pause)* We're trying to build bridges with this debate, not further increase the distance between us.

MEHROSH I'm with you on that, ma'am, but by deciding what Jai sir can or cannot ask us, you're doing exactly that.

JAI   Ladies, can we please relax for a second? I will come back at some point to address this, I promise. For now, are we clear on structure? Are we?

Pause.

BINA   That's a 'yes' for God's sake, Jai.

JAI   Great, we just have to survive an hour here, and then on to stage it is. *(Long pause)* We *will* survive, won't we?

BINA   We'll *thrive,* Jai... This is child's play compared to what I do every day. *(Pause)* Mehrosh, I notice Jai hasn't organised an on-call person for you, i.e. your Scherezade. So we can share her. Sherry?

SCHEREZADE   Mmm... I can ask Mimi or Jo, ma'am. They are free. Today I will do *your* touch-up so I will be busy/

MEHROSH I'm okay. I will just change into a salwar kameez and prepare for the event.

BINA   Scherezade will be around if you need her.

MEHROSH I doubt I'll need her, but thank you.

JAI See, Bina. The young are simple and tough.

BINA Don't mind Jai, Mehrosh, he is naive and full of clichés.

MEHROSH I've noticed.

JAI I am glad we agree on what makes me charming. All right now, this grand event awaits its event manager a.k.a me. Funny how, after I left primetime news, I am now reduced to lighting designer, furniture mover, celebrity coordinator, people pleaser/

SCHEREZADE Sir, I actually, have some immediate demands since you are the event manager/

JAI Demand-fulfiller ...

SCHEREZADE Sir, I am Scherezade, maybe you forgot my name. Mr. Jai. We need someone to bring the copper water bottles filled with electrolytes up here. I would like to talk to you outside on the stage about ma'am's exact position. I've heard she is on the right. I would like to speak with the lighting technician ASAP. Now I have found out that it's also you, so I would like to speak to you ASAP. Depending on that, we will touch up her contouring. Today ma'am will like only me to be here, so I need all the information.

JAI Bina am I going to be harassed intermittently or continuously?

BINA Eternally. Nothing you haven't been through before.

SCHEREZADE Ma'am needs some time on the mics to do her chanting and check her tone.

BINA   That's vital, Jai. The right tone of communication builds the right perception, you see. Don't you agree, Mehrosh?

Pause.

MEHROSH I'll be right here, reading.

JAI   Great, Ladies. See you soon. After you, Scherezade?

SCHEREZADE   Thanks Mr. Jai. Ma'am, I will lay out your vanity as soon as I know how you'll be seated on stage.

BINA   Thank you. Please don't stress Jai out for too long. Just till you get what you want.

SCHEREZADE and Jai leave the room. MEHROSH sits down on the sofa to read. Bina takes the chair in front of the mirror. She looks at herself for some time. She walks up to the glass window and looks at the sprawling green. Bina sighs.

BINA   Long drive here, wasn't it? I forgot how desolate the road to this place is. *(Pause)* This property belongs to Jitin's parents. My in-laws. Their dream was for us to all live here. Sitting out right here in fact – this would have been the balcony. All of us sipping coffee while their grandchildren ran around. Daylight changing to evening, as we all looked out at our own private forest. And when we didn't, they decided to turn it into a resort.

MEHROSH And you didn't live here because?

BINA   The first lesson of politics: You can't run a country from a forest.

MEHROSH You can't cut down a forest if you live in it.

BINA   I look forward to debating with you

MEHROSH When's the resort opening?

BINA   Ah who knows? They got busy with other things, other businesses – you know how it is.

MEHROSH I have no idea actually...

Pause.

BINA   You know what, let's keep the topics as they are. I'm genuinely interested in hearing what you have to say.

Pause.

MEHROSH I appreciate that, thank you.

MEHROSH goes back to her book. Pause.

MEHROSH Ma'am, isn't it uncomfortable to share this room with your 'opponent'?

BINA   I feel comfortable with you. In fact, I've wanted to talk to you in person for a long time. *(Pause)* Come on and look at this view. Your thesis on *'Historically marginalized communities in fragile ecosystems'* can wait. Fascinating title.

MEHROSH What does it matter when history is being altered as we speak?

BINA   I wish you would be open-minded. History is a point of view. *(Pause)* Won't you join me here? I don't bite. *(Pause)* The forest looks tremendous today- 'the woods are lovely, dark, and deep ...'

MEHROSH And you have promises to keep?

BINA   Oh come on, we can be friends for an hour.

MEHROSH hesitates. Then walks towards BINA, and a distant roar of a leopard is heard. MEHROSH stops, startled. BINA is unfazed.

BINA   What happened?

MEHROSH   I – I – *(Looks around.)*

BINA   Are you alright?

Pause.

MEHROSH   I'm fine. I just... Did you hear that?

BINA   Hear what? You're stressed about the debate. Sit down.

SCHEREZADE enters with copper water bottles. Earphones on. Starts laying out BINA 's vanity case. Unnecessarily loud.

BINA   Actually, drink this.

Bina takes one of the copper bottles from Scherezade's hands. This is also a moment for the light to change indicating a change in the weather.

SCHEREZADE *(on the phone)* / I would like a detailed report on the weather, sir.

MEHROSH   I'm fine, I just/

SCHEREZADE   No, I was not informed about the rain. Yes, thank you. I will wait for your update on the exact predictions. *(to Bina)* Bina ma'am, I am sorry, but there has been a very bad miscommunication about the weather's intentions. Jai sir saw big water drops fall on our heads. This is not okay. Not okay. And I'm only carrying all this stuff up here.

MEHROSH, in the meantime, has received a call. She steps towards the door but comes back soon enough.

MEHROSH   Poor signal. *(Goes close to the window. Lowering her voice)* What? I didn't give you the address

/ Who forwarded it to you? That's so strange I told you don't discuss things with Ammi, she gets...

SCHEREZADE *(raising her voice deliberately)* I am sorry ma'am. This is unaccepting. We cannot have rainfall tonight/

BINA   Call Jai. Then Fernandes at the Met Department. Then let's talk about why we didn't know about this.?

SCHEREZADE rings him while speaking. BINA, meanwhile, sends a text.

SCHEREZADE   The event will be destroyed. More than that it will change the briefing given to staff. The material of your dress, the colour, all what we pictured about your look and how you prepare and manifest your energies will go for a toss – *(Jai picks up)* Yes, Mr. Jai, we are concerned about the event vis-a-vis this climate today. Hello? Can you hear me? Could you please come up here? Thank you.

SCHEREZADE starts doing BINA 's make-up.

MEHROSH   Sameer, you cannot believe everything you hear. They're... Listen to me. I am fine. I am with very senior people, and nothing will happen. Send me a message if you can't get through.

MEHROSH looks pale. She looks out at the sprawling green.

MEHROSH *(almost to herself)* You're right, it is tremendous...

BINA   I texted Fernandes. He says they're expecting a thunderstorm for about an hour, maybe more. That's the thing about the weather, girls, it may seem like one thing, but it changes so quick you wouldn't see it coming.

MEHROSH And you're what? The oncoming storm?

BINA   Oh no my dear, I'm but one drop. Was that your brother?

SCHEREZADE Ma'am, I am extremely sorry about the storm, I will assume complete responsibility.

BINA   It's fine this time, Scherezade. Take a few numbers from me and let us find out first, what everyone else will know last. That's how we work.

Pause.

SCHEREZADE Sure ma'am, I will. Mehrosh ma'am, as Bina ma'am mentioned, I can offer you personal services for make-up today if you want.

BINA   Yes, feel free. What's mine is yours today.

MEHROSH Thank you Scherezade, but I think I'm fine. I'm just going to call home.

BINA   Absolutely, call mum and brother. Sameer, no?

Pause.

MEHROSH Yes, that's right.

SCHEREZADE Bina ma'am... A few points: you will face the camera but with your left profile. They are using mostly amber light, and it's great for all your make-up, but it will change your lip colour, but if we go with a chocolate brown for the lips it will be okay.

BINA   You know Scherezade is also a self-taught make-up artist and stylist.

MEHROSH That's great.

SCHEREZADE I used to be an influencer, and learned my own skills for the trade.

BINA Scherezade is the shining example of our next generation. Anybody can become anything.

MEHROSH Like you, ma'am. Once you were the president of the student union. And now you're here. Wasn't it you, ma'am, who asked the VC to let women in your college wear make-up and stay out late if they wanted?

BINA See, history topper you are indeed! Yes, that was me. I'm flattered you know all of this. *(Pause)* I mean it. We have, at least, that in common, don't we? Strong women's ideals? *(Pause)* But those days of struggle are done. Because we don't *need* to fight anymore.

MEHROSH We'll always need to fight ma'am.

BINA *(to SCHEREZADE)* That's enough Scherezade.

SCHEREZADE continues.

BINA I'd be happy to lend you some of my optimism, Mehrosh. *(Snaps at Scherezade)* I said enough!

SCHEREZADE Sorry ma'am.

BINA Once should be enough Scherezade, to understand. *(SCHEREZADE steps away. Pause.)* It's actually, great to see young people be active in public life. Even if they don't know what they're getting into, I like young blood.

MEHROSH Young people and what they think are important, I agree.

BINA   Would you run for office yourself? Come over to us, for example?

MEHROSH I am surprised to hear you say that.

BINA   I know a good thing when I see it. The question is, do you? *(Pause)* What did you think of the American Presidential debate last night?

MEHROSH It – it – reminded me – we – all societies – are fractured.

BINA   Concise, but generic.

MEHROSH What did you think?

Pause.

BINA   Well, I thought debates can really be entertaining.

MEHROSH That's far more generic. And that's not the point of debates – to be entertaining.

BINA   That's debatable. Why shouldn't I be entertained while engaging in something serious?

MEHROSH Entertainment is a by-product. The point of a debate is to present facts that support a real argument.

BINA   And conveniently leave out other 'facts'.

MEHROSH I think that's your mandate, actually.

BINA   That's unfair.

MEHROSH How?

BINA   I'm just saying for every fact or statistic about alarming unemployment rates there is a counter statistic about the number of jobs that *have* been created, and you don't want to acknowledge that.

MEHROSH Does it take away from the fact that the unemployment statistic still exists, that it is, in fact, alarming?

BINA I'd have to see where you're getting these figures from.

MEHROSH I thought so.

BINA There is no need to get angry because I asked to *verify a statistic*, Mehrosh.

MEHROSH I am not angry, ma'am. But I am able to see through the strategy of distracting from an already-verified statistic by a government agency by continuously questioning it.

BINA Wouldn't you want to know the same?

MEHROSH I – I would. Never mind. This loop of questions and answers is precisely how we ignore a real issue. Pretty classic.

BINA Well, I would actually, put/

MEHROSH Or one brings up a non-issue which gains traction and then feeds the news cycle conveniently.

Pause

BINA You've figured it all out, then. *(Looking at the mirror. Asking SCHEREZADE sweetly as if she didn't snap at her moments ago.)* Sheru, There is still a bit of darkness under my eyes. How can you leave it like that?

SCHEREZADE *(rushes back)* I'm sorry, ma'am.

BINA You know I don't like it when we leave our jobs unfinished, darling.

SCHEREZADE I'm sorry, ma'am.

Long pause

SCHEREZADE   Excuse me, Mehrosh ma'am, what colour is your salwar?

MEHROSH   Brown, mud brown.

SCHEREZADE   My humble advice is, if you apply lipstick, please go with nude colours...

JAI enters.

JAI   Wow, it's gotten gloomy in here. You know, we don't ever see rain this time of the year. You must have talked to Fernandes, I'll bet.

BINA   What should have happened is, he should have called us.

JAI   Ooh, I wouldn't want to be Fernandes right now.

BINA   What a waste... all this effort, getting Jitin and his family to have this room ready for all of us.

JAI   Jitin was quite compliant when we spoke, you know.

BINA   And was it his genius idea to have it outside? Or yours?

JAI   This is completely unexpected, Bina, even you know that.

SCHEREZADE   I'm sure it's unexpected sir, but I'm a little concerned how we are unable to control the weather.

Pause. Everyone except SCHEREZADE laughs.

JAI   So, it's possible we're going to be set back by a little more. But we're going to cover everything, the stage, the audience. This *is* going to happen. So please sit tight/

SCHEREZADE That means the lighting will change/

JAI I"m sure there will be some last-minute changes/

SCHEREZADE We are just not prepared, Mr. Jai.

JAI Mehrosh, do you have any questions?

MEHROSH I just think you *should* control the weather, Jai sir.

Pause.

BINA Yes, Jai sir, please.

JAI Come on/

SCHEREZADE Sir, I am serious. We have prepared for cotton clothes.

JAI Seriously?

SCHEREZADE Sir, you also know that cotton and rain is not a good combination. We may need to arrange for something that can dry fast and not look bad. Can we see her position on stage?

JAI Bina, you can't be serious.

BINA Once I hand out responsibilities, I don't second guess my staff.

SCHEREZADE We will mark it exactly so that later there is not confusion.

JAI Can we all take a moment to just breathe please? *(Pause)* Actually, that's mostly for me. Breathe, Jai, breathe.

BINA Sit down, Jai. Have a cup of tea.

SCHEREZADE I'll make for you, sir, because I will be troubling you further very soon.

JAI   / Great

BINA   / Make me one too please. Do we have almond milk here?

SCHEREZADE looks inside the fridge.

SCHEREZADE Yes. (*to MEHROSH*) Ma'am would you like one too?

BINA   She would. Normal milk?

MEHROSH Actually, I would like another space to study and also prepare for the debate? Is this possible?

JAI   Is there another useable indoor space, Bina? I doubt that there/

BINA   I told you the two big common areas are under construction. The bedrooms are now storage, and the rest... well the rest is just acres of green, Mehrosh. A kingdom unto itself. We wouldn't let you into this deep, dark forest -

JAI   We wouldn't, no no.

BINA   Although if you absolutely can't stand to be around us, my car is downstairs if you prefer to study there. My driver Michael is an angel. I can ask him to come around.

MEHROSH It's not that I can't stand... Look, that's fine, I'll just stay here.

JAI   Wow, is this Michael from – I don't know – a hundred years ago?

BINA Oh yes, he hasn't left my side. *(Pause)* In fact, on our way here, he reminded me of the time we got stuck on the expressway into the city.

JAI Six hours, was it? The longest I've been in a car not moving... Jitin and you nearly strangled each other.

BINA And then we drove right back to the city, sent Michael home and drank ourselves silly at the Cricket Club.

JAI I met Jitin at the club, recently, did he tell you?

BINA He did not.

SCHEREZADE serves them all tea, while we hear a soft drizzle outside.

SCHEREZADE It's starting. The rain.

JAI We can hear it, thank you.

MEHROSH Thank you.

A sudden spell of phone notifications. They all check their phones.

BINA Scherezade, please tell me what is going on. I can't be disturbed now.

JAI Ah Mehrosh, you tweeted about this event.

MEHROSH Yes, sorry, did you not want me to? I didn't mention anything else, just that tonight I'm in an exciting debate – I –

JAI I thought we talked about it –

BINA Invitees only, right? No gatecrashers tonight.

JAI   Exactly, I want your cheering squads out of this. Just your singular voices doing the talking like normal people.

MEHROSH   I want my people to know what I am about to do tonight.

BINA   Smart girl.

SCHEREZADE   Should we also tweet, ma'am?

BINA   Unnecessary. People who need to know where I am, already do.

SCHEREZADE   Ma'am, sir, can we look at Bina ma'am's position on stage, please? I request you.

JAI   Ma'am?

BINA   It's so gloomy outside.

JAI   Let's do this before it pours and before I lose my mind. (*Looking at Sherezade.*)

BINA, SCHEREZADE and JAI leave as SCHEREZADE looks at her phone, speaking.

SCHEREZADE   According to our sources, the weather will become worse. Ice-hail might fall. ICE-HAIL.

JAI   That's tautology.

SCHEREZADE   What?

JAI   I'll be with you in a second.

BINA   Take your time. Scherezade –!

BINA and SCHEREZADE leave.

JAI   Mehrosh, I don't understand why you tweeted about this, after I expressly said the publicity will happen after the event.

MEHROSH   I didn't know you felt strongly about it.

JAI   Really, because I think I made that clear. You also seem out of sorts and I'm/

MEHROSH I feel like I'm not in the know of everything.

JAI   What do you want to know?

MEHROSH Who are these sponsors?

JAI   What?

MEHROSH You're changing lanes for this very reason, right? So you're *independent*?

JAI   Independence means no editorial control, not no money.

MEHROSH Can you tell me who they are?

JAI   You don't trust me.

MEHROSH Sameer has been trying to get in touch. He says that – look, I'm worried, and I needed people to know what I'm doing.

JAI   Wait, are you worried about your safety? *(Pause)* Because there is nothing to be worried about. You're with me. Come down and take a look at the stage.

JAI leaves. MEHROSH looks around the room. She hears the sound of the wild cat again. She looks at her phone, and leaves in a hurry.

Empty room for a few moments. The light flickers. The sound of thunder again. Lights go off. Darkness. Soon, an emergency light comes on with occasional beeping, perhaps from a UPS. In this meagre light, we see a larger-than-life shadow of what seems like a wild cat. The shadow grows bigger, but what emerges is the shadow of a leopard. Moments pass.

Jai enters. Fumbles around in the dark. The shadow changes position, as if hiding from him. He switches his mobile phone light on.

JAI   Damn this place.

He goes towards the window with his mobile phone light. The shadow of the leopard follows him as he looks out. Finds his way to one of the chairs. Now the shadow is above him.

It looks majestic. He tries to make a call. He is unable to get through.

He is about to leave but stops. He returns to the glass window to look at the sprawling green, now grey. He smiles at it after a while, as if in deep appreciation. He receives a text.

What the hell? I knew we should have signed NDAs.

Suddenly tired he slumps into the chair.

Loosens his tie. Jai swerves in the chair, suddenly. The shadow moves in the opposite direction. Jai tries to make a call. Can't get through. Gets up. By mistake he kicks some of the make-up down. Bends to pick it up. Can't really see very much, so kicks it aside, frustrated. Makes a call again. No luck.

He stares at his phone. Looks worried. Looks at himself in the mirror with his cellphone light. He looks different – a little frightening for the first time.

JAI   Ladies and Gentlemen, welcome to absolute disaster. In one corner of the boxing ring, we have opponent number one: Bina *(imitates her)* "Call God, Jai. Be God, Jai. Make the rain stop, Jai. And now, dance, Jai." aaaaaaaand Mehrosh *(imitates her)* "Jai sir, tell me everything, sir. Now that I know everything sir, everything's a problem, sir." What do they have in common? Strong ideas, a massive Twitter following, and distinct visions. What separates them? Strong ideas, a massive Twitter following and distinct visions! What are we waiting for? Electricity apparently. Let the games begin! Let the claws come out!

SCHEREZADE enters. Half wet. The shadow becomes faint.

JAI You're soaked. Sorry, I don't know what I can offer you to dry up ... *(Looks around, but not really making an effort.)*

SCHEREZADE It's okay, sir. Don't strain. I carry a hand towel and extra things always in my bag.

SCHEREZADE goes towards her handbag behind the pillar where she first left it. JAI helps her by pointing his light where she goes. It isn't very helpful. She switches on her own cell phone light. Takes out a towel. Wipes herself.

SCHEREZADE I am in extreme panic. How are we going to have this debate? And how will Bina ma'am's touch-up be done? *(Notices the fallen make-up.)* Sir, give me some light. All the make-up is fallen down. *(Mumbling)* I left it so neatly. It's so costly these luxury products.

Jai points his cell phone light at her as she bends down to pick it all up.

JAI We have larger problems at hand.

SCHEREZADE Sir, I understand. But/

JAI Look this isn't in my control, yeah? You know I'm a journalist and not the weather god, right?

Long pause.

SCHEREZADE Sir, may I ask you something please? What is the real goal of today?

JAI   It's a *real* debate. An argument with dignity. This is my vision for my channel – I mean isn't it obvious?

SCHEREZADE No sir, it's not so obvious. That is why I am asking you.

JAI   I take it you watch TV every night?

SCHEREZADE Yes sir, I have installed two TVs which I watch together, plus there is updates from other channels on laptop every night.

JAI   How diligent. *(Pause)* We've become cheap imitations of ourselves. Our imaginations are dead. The daily news today, the thing I grew up with the utmost respect for, has become – It's as though we've gone back in time, and our reptilian brains are now at work;. the ugliest part of ourselves that we managed to suppress through civilisation and education. It's on the surface now bubbling in a dirty volcano of blood and puss.

SCHEREZADE Sir, I know you write poetry now, but frankly I cannot understand this.

Pause.

JAI *(irritated)* I just wanted two people whom I consider extremely smart in their own right, who the world sees as adversaries – and they are ideologically, of course, adversaries – to *really* speak to each other. And listen.

SCHEREZADE But sir, this is not loud like what it is on TV.

JAI   Exactly. *Exactly*! I wanted us to return to our normal register again.

SCHEREZADE   Who will watch this sir? You are not part of any news channel. Full-time.

JAI   We have so many viewers on YouTube. This is the new world. And I will make my mark here with ethics.

SCHEREZADE   Please sir, you have 100k viewers. That is very less. And that is not the voter. Your followers drink Ethiopian coffee and go to ski in Europe which is not a sport if you ask me. The voter is my mom and dad. They want to know who can speak loudly, with powerful words and with authority and give them safety in all ways.

JAI   Authority is a matter of perception. Of course, you know how perception works. For instance, the hate for Mehrosh is what you choose to see from where you stand. Do you know how many young people she inspires?

SCHEREZADE   Sir, I know very simple things, sir. I am a simple girl, who got this job I can't even dream of. It got possible by Bina ma'am, and her party's effort to make my situation better. I also know today the demand is for good packaging in news because I am young. In your channel only people like you will watch and feel great and sophisticated because/

JAI   I'm tired of this stupid argument of demand and supply. Demand better, then. BE better. Be bloody better. Stop this charade. And if sophisticated means talking with a bit of nuance and not slinging shit on each other then, yes, let's try sophistication for a change.

SCHEREZADE I don't agree, sir. People and what they need comes first.

JAI   Don't be an idiot.

Pause. SCHEREZADE's voice is shaking.

SCHEREZADE We need some lights here. This light is not enough for any work.

JAI   I'll send some over, relax. *(Pause)* I hope you've deleted the video you took of Mehrosh.

SCHEREZADE Sir, I *have*. I showed ma'am also. She complained to you?

JAI   She mentioned it. *(Pause)* Why would you *do* something like that?

SCHEREZADE Sir, she was doing some kind of yoga or some gymnastic, and she stood on her hands and almost walked on it. It was very awesome, so I thought to record/

JAI   And maybe you would have sent it 'harmlessly' to a friend or two. And suddenly one day there would be a vicious Whatsapp forward using the picture out of context.

Long pause.

SCHEREZADE Sir, you can ask Bina ma'am/

JAI   How dare you take a video of someone without their permission?

SCHEREZADE Sir, it was a mistake. I apologised a lot.

JAI   Would it be okay if I just started taking a video of you now?

SCHEREZADE Sir, it's very dark so you cannot.

JAI You – you and our entire culture need saving.

SCHEREZADE Sir, I can again apologize to Mehrosh ma'am. *(Pause)* Sir, truthfully, I can tell you this. My mother and brother and me, watched you on TV every night. We admired you. Your language and words. How you came in the same way neatly every day. We could see that you were kind and good.

JAI is surprised.

JAI Uh, thank you. *(Pause)* That was unexpected I – appreciate it/

SCHEREZADE But the truth is, *you* don't care about people like me. You like girls like Mehrosh. Who are able to speak the same things in the same language and words as yours/

JAI *That* is an unfounded accusation. Mehrosh isn't from wealth or the 'sophistication' you seem to grudge. So tell me, why does she decide to do something extraordinary and the rest of you... just...

SCHEREZADE Because we are not the same people and our families are different and we come in different packets, sir. Like biscuits. Anyway, I know to you we are good as audience but if we come close to you – *(Pause)* Anyway, we need lights here, sir. I'll ask the team for candles. But you can kindly arrange a more modern solution and give us the event ETA.

JAI I'm on it.

SCHEREZADE Otherwise we may not be able to participate.

JAI   Oh please, I'll have light here, Scherezade. Don't you worry. *(Pause)* You can really be better than this.

SCHEREZADE Sir, you can also be better.

JAI   What?

SCHEREZADE *(her voice shaking)* That only.

JAI exits exasperated. SCHEREZADE sits alone in the dark as the shadow of the leopard fades. Now, her shadow is quite small. MEHROSH enters. SCHEREZADE shrieks.

MEHROSH It's me – God –

SCHEREZADE I got scared.

MEHROSH Did you see something?

SCHEREZADE I saw you.

MEHROSH Yes, I know. Because I'm here. *(Pause)* I feel like there is – Never mind. *(Looking at her closely)* Have you been crying?

SCHEREZADE Too much pressure for me, and Jai sir is not helping me. *(Pause)* Also, ma'am, I would like to apologise for all this video confusion.

MEHROSH There is no confusion, Scherezade.

SCHEREZADE Sorry ma'am. I can really offer you my services to do a small make-up job as a gift.

MEHROSH I'm going to change in the bathroom.

SCHEREZADE Ma'am, no light there. Floor is also little wet. I'll just turn around and close my eyes. Do it here.

MEHROSH I'll carry my phone as a light.

SCHEREZADE You'll spoil your outfit.

MEHROSH Fine. Put your phone face down and turn around.

SCHEREZADE does as she's told. As she watches SCHEREZADE, MEHROSH pulls out her clothing: a salwar kameez, dainty. As she changes into it, her body in the shadow reveals her musculature, her athletic body.

SCHEREZADE That's a very beautiful dress, ma'am... *(Pause)* I mean it.

MEHROSH Thank you. My mother got it stitched for me last birthday.

SCHEREZADE I have a good lipstick for this. Just try it. You can put it on your own.

MEHROSH I need an eye pencil also. Forgot to pack mine.

SCHEREZADE Sure ma'am. Can you give me some light in this bag? *(MEHROSH holds a light while SCHEREZADE searches the vanity laid out on the table. Hands her the lipstick.)* I think this shade will suit it.

MEHROSH Thanks. *(Applies lipstick and eye pencil)* That's it. That's how I get ready. Were you always interested in make-up or did you learn it for this job?

SCHEREZADE Bina ma'am told you right? I used to run a budget fashion and beauty blog. You can go see, some videos are still there. Actually, that was how I got the job with Bina ma'am. I made a video about my brother, who is fully in a wheelchair trying to go into some buildings and stations in the city. It got the attention of our local representative who constructed ramps for the area.

MEHROSH Why did you stop making videos?

SCHEREZADE Because it was not a real job, ma'am. My family needs steady income.

MEHROSH And why –?

SCHEREZADE Why I took a job with politics? *(She takes off her left glove and reveals her hand which has a large burn mark. Its shadow looks large, monstrous, grotesque.)* In some 'normal' workplaces, they will ask me to take off my glove and look at my scar like it is something horrible. It's just a hand ma'am.

They both look at the large shadow of the hand.

MEHROSH It's actually, quite – beautiful.

SCHEREZADE Ma'am, you are very polite. You are doing good in this country.

MEHROSH Sometimes I think I am an advertisement for what not to do if you want a normal life. *(Pause)* I was fascinated by your name. Scherezade.

SCHEREZADE It's a posh name, right? Someone with money. Which I am not.

MEHROSH Or you're the girl who saved her life by telling a thousand and one stories. *(Pause) The Arabian Nights?*

SCHEREZADE No...

The shadows change. SCHEREZADE and MEHROSH look like two small girls in the shadow.

MEHROSH Scherezade marries this king Sharyar, despite her father's wishes. Sharyar believed that his first wife was unfaithful to him. He decided that all women were the same. And so for revenge, he married a new virgin every day and after their first night together, he'd kill the woman off. Then he could be sure she would never betray him. You know, basically never have sex with someone else. You understand, right?

SCHEREZADE Ya obviously, ma'am.

MEHROSH So Scherezade – I think she is his minister's daughter? She says she will marry him. And then each night she tells him a story. The story is just, just, captivating, but by dawn she says that she can only continue it the next night. And so he spares her. And she does this for a thousand and one nights. And then at the end, he falls in love with her, and she marries this madman.

SCHEREZADE Wow. What a story. *(Pause)* My parents – they adopted me. This name was on my dress, and the orphanage said to please keep this name. It was a request from my original parents. My current parents are humble people. And good family. So they kept the name.

MEHROSH That's interesting.

SCHEREZADE Yes, I am also like that Scherezade I can tell nice stories.

Thunder. They are both startled. A purring. They have both clearly heard it. They just look at each other in silence, both aware that the other has heard it. Scherezade is quick to shake it off.

MEHROSH Did you ever try to find your... your birth parents?

SCHEREZADE Never. It doesn't matter for me.

MEHROSH You said your brother's using a wheelchair?

SCHEREZADE My brother is born like this. My parents didn't want to risk one more 'bad baby', so they did this adoption. Of me. After a few days itself, there was a fire in the house. My bed caught fire and also my hair and hand, but they saved me in time before it could become worse. We lost all our things, my family struggled quite a lot after that to make it up. *(Pause)* They didn't say it very often, but I was considered unlucky. I couldn't get a job or anything because of it –

MEHROSH That isn't right –

SCHEREZADE Once one CEO of a vegan cupcake company told me to take my glove off, and then she called all the people in the office to see it. Her behaviour inspired me to start this channel online. Talking honestly about issues. I got nearly 500K followers, and see ma'am, now I am here.

MEHROSH Good for you, Scherezade ...

SCHEREZADE But... *(Pause)* But, what ma'am? You are thinking something.

MEHROSH But, okay... tell me what do you really think about what is happening in the country today?

SCHEREZADE My opinion doesn't matter, ma'am.

MEHROSH It does. Everyone's opinion matters.

Pause.

SCHEREZADE The only person who thought I was not an unlucky person, for who my opinion matters, was Bina ma'am. That's why I am here.

MEHROSH Okay, tell me. Your name is Scherezade, right? Tomorrow if there is a riot and you are asked for your name, and – and – something terrible happens to you only because of your name, wouldn't that just be so heartbreaking?

SCHEREZADE Yes, but then I was nobody. Now I can call Bina ma'am/

MEHROSH Just imagine it for one second, okay. Just for the heck of it. It's the middle of the night. You're going back from an event like this on a desolate road... Your car is stopped. You're alone, and you're asked/

SCHEREZADE What about the driver?

MEHROSH The driver is also pulled out, and the men who've stopped you have petrol cans and baseball bats. And you are asked your *name.*

SCHEREZADE I will tell them my full name and it won't be a problem.

MEHROSH Don't you think the very idea that this could happen, that you imagined it instantly without much difficulty – itself is wrong?

SCHEREZADE Yes it is, ma'am. But this is because people can be bad. I can get stopped by – a different kind of crowd. I have to change my answer then. Say something which is okay for them. But anyway, it won't happen to us/

MEHROSH Oh no, *I* could get stopped. They could pull me out, and recognise my face, and the things they say to me online – the rape threats and the death threats could be real in a moment.

SCHEREZADE No ma'am. You are too public for this. It will not/

MEHROSH I don't think you understand. They can come for us. Anything can be a problem for anyone – gender, religion, the size of your head. Even some day you, Scherezade, with your funny name and your odd story will be a problem to someone, and you can be dispensed with.

SCHEREZADE If you mean they will throw me out, I'll try to go abroad before that, ma'am/

MEHROSH That's not the answer. So all I hear is: I don't think there is anything wrong with this country. / But I have *still* made plans to go abroad.

SCHEREZADE Everyone has to have some plans no ma'am/

MEHROSH And the reason for me to emigrate someday is because I *know* I'm contributing to making this country eventually unliveable, so it doesn't matter what happens to the rest. What an unimaginative and cowardly argument. I am tired of people like you.

Pause.

SCHEREZADE Even Jai sir is tired of me. *(Pause)* Maybe I am like that girl from that story. I am just trying to save my life.

Long pause.

MEHROSH Do you know why she marries the mad king? So that she can put a stop to the senseless butchering of other women.

SCHEREZADE gets up to take a few steps.

The shadow of the leopard goes past them quickly. They both register the movement of it.

MEHROSH You can't run into the bathroom every time you're confronted Scherezade. And you cannot ignore that something just moved here.

SCHEREZADE I didn't see anything.

Pause.

MEHROSH Can I see your phone please? I know you said you deleted it.

SCHEREZADE Ma'am I did.

MEHROSH Then let's see it.

MEHROSH reaches for SCHEREZADE's phone, who tightens her grip on it.

SCHEREZADE I have a lot of important stuff of Bina ma'am.

MEHROSH   You can hold it. Just show me your gallery.

SCHEREZADE and MEHROSH look at each other for a long time. The shadow of the leopard is now very present in the room. SCHEREZADE shows the phone is still tightly in her grip.

MEHROSH Tell me you've heard the sounds too?

SCHEREZADE *(looking straight into her eyes)* No ma'am. Your mind is playing tricks.

MEHROSH Show me your phone. *(SCHEREZADE grips her phone even tighter. Slowly she extends her hand. MEHROSH goes through it. MEHROSH looks at her for a long time. The sound of the rain increases.)* You didn't delete all of them.

SCHEREZADE You can delete them. *(MEHROSH deletes them.)* Happy?

MEHROSH *Happy?*

SCHEREZADE I wasn't going to use them or anything.

MEHROSH You lied.

SCHEREZADE I'm sorry. I will go check what is ETA of the debate.

SCHEREZADE is about to leave the room. The leopard purrs from very close by. MEHROSH looks around, startled. SCHEREZADE is unfazed.

SCHEREZADE I like tricks.

Just as SCHEREZADE is about to leave, BINA enters.

BINA   You're leaving?

Pause.

SCHEREZADE Ma'am -

BINA   I need a touch-up.

MEHROSH I – I – I need some air.

BINA   Outside you'll get just water. *(Pause)* Jai said you could go downstairs in ten minutes for a quick picture. I just did mine.

Bina sits in front of the mirror. SCHEREZADE gets ready to do her touch-up.

BINA   So what were you girls talking about?

MEHROSH Immigration.

MEHROSH switches on her cell light and goes into the bathroom.

SCHEREZADE Nothing – Mehrosh ma'am told me the story of *Arabian Nights*.

BINA   Ha! All thousand and one of them?

SCHEREZADE TLDR ma'am. *(Looking at her phone)* Jitin sir tried calling me. Did he try calling you?

BINA   I don't want to speak with him right now.

SCHEREZADE Should I tell him that?

BINA   What do you think? *(Still looking at her phone.)*

SCHEREZADE Ma'am he messaged saying – saying – *(shows BINA the phone while whispering)*

BINA   What?

SCHEREZADE He sent it this morning.

BINA   Just tell him I'll talk to him when I get home.

SCHEREZADE starts to type a message.

SCHEREZADE Ma'am, he says...

BINA   And tell him that he shouldn't be getting my *assistant* to convince me of children.

SCHEREZADE *(typing furiously)* I'm writing it, ma'am/

BINA   Tell him that I don't have a maternal cell in my body. They were all destroyed after –

Suddenly aware that MEHROSH is in the bathroom. Lowers her voice.

SCHEREZADE *(reading aloud as she types)* Ma'am doesn't have maternal cells in her body/

BINA   And his parents. Only fixated on their lineage. Now they're suddenly okay for us to adopt. Couldn't we have considered it before my body went through hell?

MEHROSH comes out of the bathroom.

SCHEREZADE Ma'am, I really think adoption is a good idea.

Pause.

MEHROSH Do you both want some privacy?

BINA   Not at all, Mehrosh.

SCHEREZADE Not at all Mehrosh, ma'am. Will you adopt ma'am if you couldn't have children?

MEHROSH I'm not sure I want children/

SCHEREZADE Bina ma'm is so brave. You remember when she told all of the city's children, were her children? Then in the rally all the street kids came running to her calling her their mother. That was an epic moment. 'Ma, Mummy, Mama!' they were shouting, and you should have seen Jitin sir's mom's face just shocked at the smell and the... Her in-laws got so screwed after all the pestering of having children. I still remember – they troubled her so much I thought ma'am and me both finished – out of the house...

BINA   Go on Scherezade. Do go on.

Pause.

BINA   I had three miscarriages. But then I got higher up in the party. So I stayed.

MEHROSH I think I should go down for the photograph now.

MEHROSH leaves.

SCHEREZADE Ma'am, I'm very sorry to ask you this, but what should I tell Jitin sir exactly?

BINA   Scherezade if you don't know, you shouldn't be here. *(Pause)* I have to look good.

SCHEREZADE You will, you will, I promise. Come ma'am, let's do your touch up.

SCHEREZADE puts on her phone torch light. To which Bina adds hers. They manage to create some light in which SCHEREZADE can set the finishing touches on

Bina's hair and make-up. Bina plays some meditation music on her phone. The sonorous quality of the music makes it seem quite ominous.

BINA   This is my opening statement. Listen: They say the mark of a great nation is its young – what they dream of, what they think is possible/

SCHEREZADE *(softly)* Ma'am, you can tilt your face?

BINA moves as directed by SCHEREZADE.

BINA   Let me tell you a story. I met a young girl once. She had a kind of deformity from birth. A kind of disability, you could say. *(Scherezade pauses)* She ran a Youtube channel, while also trying to find a job, but she wouldn't get one, because of the prejudices surrounding her. Her family depended on her. Her brother, who was in a wheelchair, was on the brink of suicide.

SCHEREZADE stops for a second.

BINA   She managed to reach out to us through her channel and apart from building twenty-eight ramps in the neighbourhood, we also gave her a job. Now she has bought a house for her family, she runs social media for us, makes a good living, her brother/

SCHEREZADE Ma'am, turn that side.

Pause.

SCHEREZADE He did not commit suicide, ma'am. And I still didn't buy the house.

BINA   This is biographical fiction, Scherezade. And I said *brink*. It means almost. *(Pause)* You take something factual, and you add a very probable reality to it. We have to tell your story Scherezade. In a way that people will get it. We are given some things. We take them, and we make them work for us. Whatever they are. Do you understand this? *(SCHEREZADE nods.)* I took my miscarriages, and I traded the pain for power. You took your hand and you traded it for this life. *(Pause)* Show me your hand. Show me. *(SCHEREZADE offers it to her hesitantly.)* Don't be ashamed of it. It's this hand Scherezade that made me want to take you in. It held you back at first, but it is now your ticket to heaven. The greatest work I've ever done in faith, is you. And that's why I will tell your story. *(They look at each other for a long time. SCHEREZADE bows down to touch BINA's feet. BINA touches her head, and then asks her to get up.)*

SCHEREZADE Ma'am, why don't people like Mr. Jai like me? Why do they think I am disgusting?

BINA   Because they don't know anything. They think power is in words and speeches and books. Power is in people like you.

Pause.

BINA   Now, can we please get back to my face?

SCHEREZADE is a bit emotional as she finishes the touch-ups on Bina's face.

SCHEREZADE Sometimes I feel like your daughter, ma'am.

BINA   Only blood can be family Scherezade. *(Pause)* Orphans never truly belong anywhere.

JAI and MEHROSH enter with candles. The room lights up a little more and now we see four shadows of the people on stage.

JAI   Bina, your staff downstairs is going beserk. None of them have cellular signal. They can't understand why I am personally carrying candles to your room even though you have an entourage. Maybe they think they've lost their jobs?

BINA   They accept and honour that I am very particular about who I share space with, Jai. Today is not their day. It's Mehrosh's, in fact. Mehrosh, did you take a good picture?

MEHROSH I did. *(Pause)* The stage is smaller than I thought.

JAI   Intimate, M. Cosy, more like.

BINA   It's cosy here too, Jai. So cosy we're barely able to see each other.

JAI   Yes, yes, madam, I brought candles. Old school solutions to the rescue!

JAI and MEHROSH hand out candles to BINA and SCHEREZADE. A short silence.

JAI   Ladies, if you think about it, it's a rather extraordinary day with extraordinary people, despite the hurdles. I couldn't have imagined sharing this time with you, this way. Thank you, Bina, for germinating the idea.

BINA   Of course.

MEHROSH There are more candles. Maybe we should light a few more?

In silence, all four of them light candles. The light changes. Their shadows are large now. The sound of the rain pelting down continues.

SCHEREZADE It's like a birthday without a cake.

MEHROSH I was going to say it's like a candlelight vigil.

BINA   Birthdays are more cheerful.

JAI   Actually, let's wish for something. Come on? *(Pause)* It's my wish that whatever happens in our great nation, may we continue to be decent. And please let the rain not ruin this new endeavour.

MEHROSH Inshallah. May we honour our constitution and the spirit of education. May we preserve all life and all forests.

SCHEREZADE I wish to be with my brother on his birthday.

BINA   May we change our minds if we need to. May we know what is good for us.

Another long moment of silence.

JAI   I'm reminded of a – a – remember that night, Bina?

BINA   Which night?

JAI   We were all out here – when this was a terrace – we had a party for the alumni – and we heard something.

BINA   One hears a lot of things when old classmates are drinking single malts.

MEHROSH What did you hear?

JAI   Well, some years before that, we were driving here actually, to meet Bina's in-laws – they'd just closed the deal on this place – and we found a wounded leopard. Right here on the highway outside this property. It was in a near-death situation, bleeding – just terrible. Right Bina?

BINA   Yes. It just came out of nowhere.

JAI   It was – it was –

BINA   It wasn't your fault, Jai. It was a freak accident in the dark. You slammed the brakes as hard as you could when you saw it –

JAI   We shouldn't have been driving. And I certainly shouldn't have taken the wheel. It was just the euphoria of having signed the resort deal, getting the permissions, rushing back to tell Uncle and Aunty we were ready.

BINA   You still don't expect a leopard on your way –

MEHROSH What happened to it?

BINA   Well, we lifted it up, put it in the car and brought it here. We had a vet come – it was nursed – she was – back to life. And my in-laws were going to send it to a National Park/

MEHROSH But they didn't?

BINA   They intended to.

JAI   For a few days that it was there, they had it, her, it was a leopardess, in a cage in their living room, for people to come witness this – and it – her – became a sort of thing. A strange thing. People would be eating and drinking while this animal just sat caged in the middle of the living room. I think Uncle and Aunty got carried away for a short while.

MEHROSH And?

BINA   I know, but it lived. It escaped.

JAI   It lived. It lived, indeed.

MEHROSH 's phone beeps with texts for a few moments.

BINA   Are we set, Jai? How many people are we expecting?

JAI   I've been told a number of our invitees are in the outhouse at the front gate. There are two hundred more than we expected. Security are holding them back. So we're a bit delayed.

SCHEREZADE So your number has tripled? Why?

JAI   Well, because the damn address was leaked.

SCHEREZADE How sir? How did that happen?

BINA   Don't question my staff, Jai. They have strict orders to keep it as private as you wanted.

SCHEREZADE But now if it is leaked, I can do some socials from ma'am's private –

JAI   Absolutely not.

MEHROSH *(on her phone)* I've told some friends from university to come.

JAI   What?

MEHROSH I invited some friends to your resort. The address was leaked. What do you expect?

JAI   The opposite of what we wanted, Mehrosh, the opposite.

BINA   She wants some friends around. Let her have that.

MEHROSH Thank you ma'am, for bestowing that on me.

BINA   I hope they're well-behaved and not an unruly mob.

MEHROSH 's phone beeps again. MEHROSH looks at her phone and walks away to make a call. The downpour has significantly increased.

SCHEREZADE It has become noisy here.

JAI   A real fan of the obvious/

SCHEREZADE That means it's going to be noisy on the stage also.

JAI   We can add floor mics if needed.

BINA   Assume they're needed and add them.

MEHROSH comes back towards them.

BINA   You look worried, Mehrosh.

SCHEREZADE *(looking at her phone)* Ma'am Jitin sir is asking what time you will reach so you can schedule a talk about the – the –

BINA glares at SCHEREZADE.

MEHROSH's phone beeps. She reads a message and walks close to the window. Her manner is slightly more frantic now.

BINA   Scherezade, did you bring my rose oil?

MEHROSH goes towards Jai and says something to him very softly.

SCHEREZADE I'm sure I did, ma'am/

BINA   It should have been laid out.

SCHEREZADE scrambles for the perfume.

JAI   That's ridiculous. Who is sending Sameer this nonsense?

MEHROSH Jai sir, I just told you privately, never mind/

BINA   What's the matter with you two now?

JAI   Mehrosh, it's not possible – it's malicious, this rumour, it's meant to scare you. Bina, her brother messaged her saying she is going to be attacked tonight.

BINA   That's absolute rubbish.

SCHEREZADE drops the bottle of rose oil. A heavy fragrance. Everyone is startled.

BINA   *Scherezade!* What is wrong with you?

SCHEREZADE I'm sorry–

JAI   Blow out your candle!

MEHROSH I – I – Jai, you don't get it. Ma'am I didn't want you to get involved – I –

SCHEREZADE I'm sorry, I'm sorry I will clean this, I –

MEHROSH It's easy for you to say... I am in the public eye in a hateful way – the rumours of an attack are real for me. I don't come with security detail.

BINA   Don't slip, please...

SCHEREZADE Please don't move, please...

SCHEREZADE is bent over and moving between them with paper towels trying to clean the floor.

BINA   Take my security, Mehrosh, I'll be fine.

A low purr as the shadow moves across the room.

JAI   Be careful, M, you'll slip. Call Sameer, I want to talk to him now. He is being an idiot by feeding you the vitriol of the hate machine.

BINA   Sameer – he is also getting involved a lot in student politics, isn't he? Smart boy, but maybe tell him to spend more time in the classroom and less on the streets/

MEHROSH   What are you trying to say?

JAI   Come on, Bina.

BINA   Jai, it's well-meaning advice. The boy seems a bit frazzled about everything -

JAI   Mehrosh, I'd say focus on the opening statement/

Another purr and the shadow leaps.

MEHROSH   There – There – did you–?

SCHEREZADE   I'm sorry, everybody, please be careful.

JAI   Mehrosh, you cannot believe these rumours. I have to go downstairs now, and check up on the power situation...

SCHEREZADE   I'm done, it's almost very clean/

BINA   If I got any on my clothes, it's going to be the end of everything. Especially you... *(to Scherezade)*

MEHROSH   Jai sir, it's been here since I got here.

JAI   I need you to stay calm. I know these rumours can be scary, but you know better –

JAI leaves. SCHEREZADE follows him out.

BINA   Rumours circulate at appalling speeds these days.

MEHROSH   Would *you* have any idea how?

BINA   *S*ounds like an accusation, when all I've done is/

MEHROSH   Let's be honest, you've – you've –

BINA   Say it, you've been wanting to say/

MEHROSH You've terrorised and surveilled and incarcerated us.

BINA   You were brought here and taken back in a private car, and that's how you feel/

MEHROSH'S phone rings. She can't recognise the number but picks up and goes towards the window.

MEHROSH Who are you? That's sick... pathetic to call and threaten me like this.

She checks her phone and is alarmed. Bina looks at her phone too.

BINA   I'm sorry, I hear they've been calling Sameer a terrorist on TV tonight.

MEHROSH What?

BINA   They've found some links to an extremist organization.

MEHROSH That's a lie/

BINA   They say they have proof –

MEHROSH So you knew – you knew – that's why –

A stone comes through the window shattering the glass, almost aimed at MEHROSH. It lands next to her feet. A small part of the big glass window shatters. The sound of the rain gets louder because of that. MEHROSH goes to pick up the stone. There is a large looming shadow of the leopard behind her. She stands frozen for a second facing the broken window and looking at the stone. She lifts the stone as if to throw it back through the glass.

MEHROSH A stone came for me through the window.

BINA   It didn't come for you. It just happened.

MEHROSH It's a suspicious evening overall, wouldn't you say?

BINA Very strange occurrences.

Pause.

MEHROSH Why are they doing this? Why are they calling him these things?

BINA I don't own the media, Mehrosh.

MEHROSH You don't?

BINA There won't be any going back, Mehrosh, if you don't stop now. (*Pause*) Look, I can't undo the news, but I can tell you that he should lay low. There are all kinds of conflicts in campuses and it's better he is not embroiled in that –

MEHROSH Should I also be careful?

BINA You're special, Mehrosh. You're smart and you're eloquent and you have a future.

MEHROSH And he doesn't?

BINA Who is going to take care of your mother if both of you are doing work like this? And perhaps your brother and you *need* someone to watch over you.

Pause.

MEHROSH We don't need anyone. We have our ammi.

BINA Anisa, right?

Pause.

MEHROSH So you know everything?

BINA It must have been difficult for her to bring you both up alone when he left so early on?

MEHROSH He didn't leave. (*Pause*)

BINA   We've watched you on TV – Jitin and I. It's admirable how dignified you look in front of all these people frothing at the mouth. *(Pause)* What a pity for a young, attractive girl like you to be in this position/

MEHROSH What position? The one you put me in?

BINA   Wouldn't you rather be like other girls your age? Take selfies or something.

MEHROSH *(snaps)* I take selfies, ma'am. Let's take one now.

BINA   Oh, I'm not sure that will help either of us.

MEHROSH is in tears. She tries to send a text.

BINA   I know that your home was not an ideal place – I can guide you, Mehrosh...

MEHROSH Nothing you can say, ma'am, or nothing you know about my family, my brother, my mother, will ever change how I feel about you, your politics, your ethics –

Phone rings. She cuts it.

BINA   Tell me, Mehrosh, what is it that is so despicable about my politics, my ethics?

MEHROSH This theatre of horror you've unleashed... I hate fear. I – I– hate fear. I hate it I hate it I hate it!

BINA   Be careful, you're walking close to the window/

MEHROSH I need to go... I have to go. I can't be here. -

Phone rings again.

MEHROSH Ammi, Hi. What did they want? Okay, listen, call Anna, she... She is a lawyer, and she does a lot of pro bono work, just do it. It's a scare tactic, but just... The police is at my mother's place.

BINA I can have this go away in a minute. Say the word.

MEHROSH just stares at her.

BINA I can make it go away, Mehrosh. You just have to come here – come to where I stand.

MEHROSH I could never...

BINA Where I am, is without fear. I can see and hear everything all the time. Like a rockstar. Like a god.

MEHROSH Really, is it that divine? Blood everywhere?

BINA Oh please Mehrosh, there isn't blood everywhere.

MEHROSH And the people who shed it are people who believe in you.

BINA Yes, we have believers. But we don't want innocent lives to be taken. Not yours, not your brother's or mother's. Nobody's, especially not yours.

Walking towards MEHROSH. MEHROSH moving closer and closer to the window.

MEHROSH Don't come close to me!

Bina stops.

BINA Why can't you just accept we are doing something brilliant? *(Shadows change.)* I was at a rally a few months ago. A hundred-year-old widow, who looked smaller than a ten-year-old child, asked to be carried to me. She told me for the first time in all her existence, a whole century, she feels like she has been awarded dignity. That her identity was affirmed. She pricked her finger with my earring and put a drop of blood on my forehead. This is real. This is devotion. This is service. *(She has tears in her eyes.)* Mehrosh, you are special. You are chosen. I see it because I am it.

MEHROSH   I don't want to die.

BINA   I know, my darling. You won't die.

MEHROSH is weeping. Bina moves closer.

BINA   You *can* come with us. You can choose us. We will never die. Our bodies may, but when we fall, we will fall into the open arms of the crowds. There will be millions of them, chanting our names, dizzy with life – carrying us to our salvation, into the purest white light. Each one burning with fire for our vision. There is no jannat in the afterlife, Mehrosh, only this – only this –

MEHROSH   It's a lie... these people who are carrying you... they are half-dead and mutilated. Their limbs are hanging by a thread, their minds are shrunk because they have no air to breathe, no water to drink, nothing to eat, and if they aren't dead, they are dying – you are being carried by the dead and the dying -

BINA   Open your eyes and see, you stupid girl!

MEHROSH   Please don't hurt my family. Please – please – don't hurt me or my family!

BINA   What family, Mehrosh? Your brother is being arrested, your poor mother... your father who left - / we can't bring him back -

MEHROSH   He didn't leave – he didn't leave!

BINA   What else do you call it, Mehrosh?

MEHROSH   Disappearing.

The roar is heard. So close, it's frightening. Bina goes close to her to pull her away from the window. MEHROSH and Bina look at each other for a second. MEHROSH holds Bina's shoulders and brings her to the floor in a neat, precise way. MEHROSH's hands are on BINA's neck for a brief second. BINA suddenly appears weak beside MEHROSH's athletic body. MEHROSH's shadow looks like she is an animal too, with all fours on the ground, looking ahead into the sprawling green. The leopard appears clearly this time for a brief second, and it's gone before the shadows of the forest appear inside the room – the walls seemingly collapsed.

The phone continues blinking.

MEHROSH looks into the audience for the first time. With fear, backing away from them too. In sheer desperation, she gets into a handstand and walks on her hands as if to expel all her energy. She manages to walk in the handstand longer than before. BINA recovers a bit, breathless and shaken. The electricity returns.

MEHROSH I – I –

MEHROSH, jolted out of this trance, rushes to pull BINA up, and quickly pours BINA a glass of water. BINA drinks in silence. Long moments pass.

MEHROSH I am so sorry. I –

BINA   We never have to talk about this.

BINA sends a text from her phone.

BINA   It's taken care of. Whatever is happening at your house.

MEHROSH Thank you? Bina, I'm sorry. I wouldn't have - you know that. I am sorry.

BINA   You are very strong. I was surprised... I saw an ancient fear in your eyes. *(Silence)* I won't tell anyone.

MEHROSH Why not?

BINA   Because you're chosen.

MEHROSH Why do you think I'm chosen?

BINA   Go wash your face, Mehrosh.

MEHROSH goes into the bathroom, while Bina sits alone looking at the mirror. MEHROSH comes out. She goes to the dresser to redo her face.

MEHROSH Did you ever see the leopard in the living room?

BINA   I did. She was beautiful.

MEHROSH Did they like having it there?

BINA   Wouldn't you? The strongest, most elegant wild animal right there for all your friends to see.

MEHROSH It must have been so scared – so so afraid for its life.

BINA   Maybe fear is at the heart of love.

MEHROSH Love is at the heart of love, no?

BINA   At this point, let's just agree to disagree.

SCHEREZADE enters.

SCHEREZADE The stage is set, and now that the power is back, we are ready for you. Do you need anything? *(softly)* Bina ma'am, are you okay? You are looking... are you feeling okay?

Pause.

BINA I'm fine Scherezade. I just got carried away with Mehrosh. I'm very pleased to inform you that Mehrosh and I are very, very good friends now. Isn't that correct?

MEHROSH Yes, we are friends.

SCHEREZADE Okay. That's good news. Are you both ready?

BINA I am. There are so many burning issues to discuss. *(Pause)* See you out there.

SCHEREZADE What happened here?

MEHROSH *(looking straight at SCHEREZADE)* Do you think fear is at the heart of love?

SCHEREZADE I –

MEHROSH Tell me you saw it. You heard it right?

SCHEREZADE Ma'am I...

MEHROSH Scherezade, look me in the eyes and tell me you see and hear it.

Long pause.

SCHEREZADE Every day, Mehrosh. *(Pause)* You have to go down, ma'am. The stage is waiting.

MEHROSH doesn't leave.

MEHROSH I want to borrow –

As if anticipating it, SCHEREZADE hands her the eye pencil.

MEHROSH uses it but doesn't leave and continues looking at herself in the mirror.

The leopard roars. SCHEREZADE is startled. Shortly after, it appears briefly. They both look at the leopard and the lights dim. The sound of thunder.

The end.

Aurora Metro Books

ADA by Emily Holyoake
ISBN 978-1-912430-09-3   £9.99

THREE WOMEN by Matilda Velevitch
ISBN 978-1-912430-35-2   £9.99

PROJECT XXX by Kim Wiltshire & Paul Hine
ISBN 978-1-906582-55-5   £8.99

COMBUSTION by Asif Khan
ISBN 978-1-911501-91-6   £9.99

DIARY OF A HOUNSLOW GIRL by Ambreen Razia
ISBN 978-0-9536757-9-1   £8.99

SPLIT/MIXED by Ery Nzaramba
ISBN 978-1-911501-97-8   £10.99

A GIRL WITH A BOOK by Nick Wood
ISBN 978-1-910798-61-4   £12.99

THE TROUBLE WITH ASIAN MEN by Sudha Bhuchar, Kristine Landon-Smith and Louise Wallinger
ISBN 978-1-906582-41-8   £8.99

WOMEN OF ASIA by Asa Palomera
ISBN 978-1-906582-94-4   £7.99

HARVEST by Manjula Padmanabhan
ISBN 978-0-9536757-7-7   £6.99

I HAVE BEFORE ME A REMARKABLE DOCUMENT by Sonja Linden
ISBN 978-0-9546912-3-3   £7.99

NEW SOUTH AFRICAN PLAYS ed. Charles J. Fourie
ISBN 978-0-9542330-1-3   £11.99

BLACK AND ASIAN PLAYS Anthology introduced by Afia Nkrumah
ISBN 978-0-9536757-4-6   £12.99

SOUTHEAST ASIAN PLAYS ed. Cheryl Robson and Aubrey Mellor
ISBN 978-1-906582-86-9   £16.99

SIX PLAYS BY BLACK AND ASIAN WOMEN WRITERS ed. Kadija George
ISBN 978-0-9515877-2-0   £12.99

www.aurorametro.com